SCHIRMER'S LIBRARY
OF MUSICAL CLASSICS

FRANZ LISZT

Rhapsodies Hongroises

For the Piano

Edited by

RAFAEL JOSEFFY

IN TWO BOOKS

→ Book I (Nos. 1- 8) — Library Vol. 1033

Book II (Nos. 9-15) — Library Vol. 1034

G. SCHIRMER, Inc.

DISTRIBUTED BY

HAL•LEONARD® CORPORATION

7777 W. BLUEMOUND RD. P.O. BOX 13819 MILWAUKEE, WI 53213

A son ami E. Zerdahely

Rhapsodie hongroise Nº 1

Edited and revised by
Rafael Joseffy

Fr. Liszt

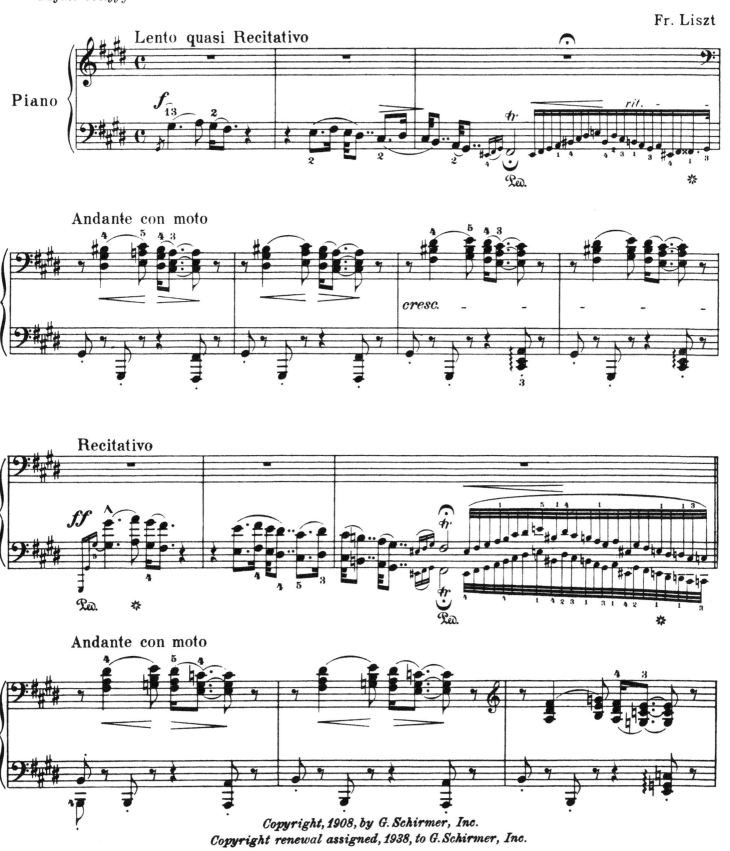

Copyright, 1908, by G. Schirmer, Inc.
Copyright renewal assigned, 1938, to G. Schirmer, Inc.
Newly-revised Edition
Copyright, 1914, by G. Schirmer, Inc.
Printed in the U.S.A.

Andante (assai moderato)

un poco ritenuto il tempo e sempre rubato

Più moderato

poco a poco più f

il basso più marcato

sempre più rinforz. e stringendo

Au Comte Ladislas Teleky

Rhapsodie hongroise Nº 2

Edited and fingered by
Rafael Joseffy

FRANZ LISZT

Piano

Lassan

Copyright, 1902, by G. Schirmer Inc.
Copyright renewal assigned, 1930, to G. Schirmer Inc.
Newly-revised Edition
Copyright, 1914, by G. Schirmer Inc.
Printed in the U. S. A.

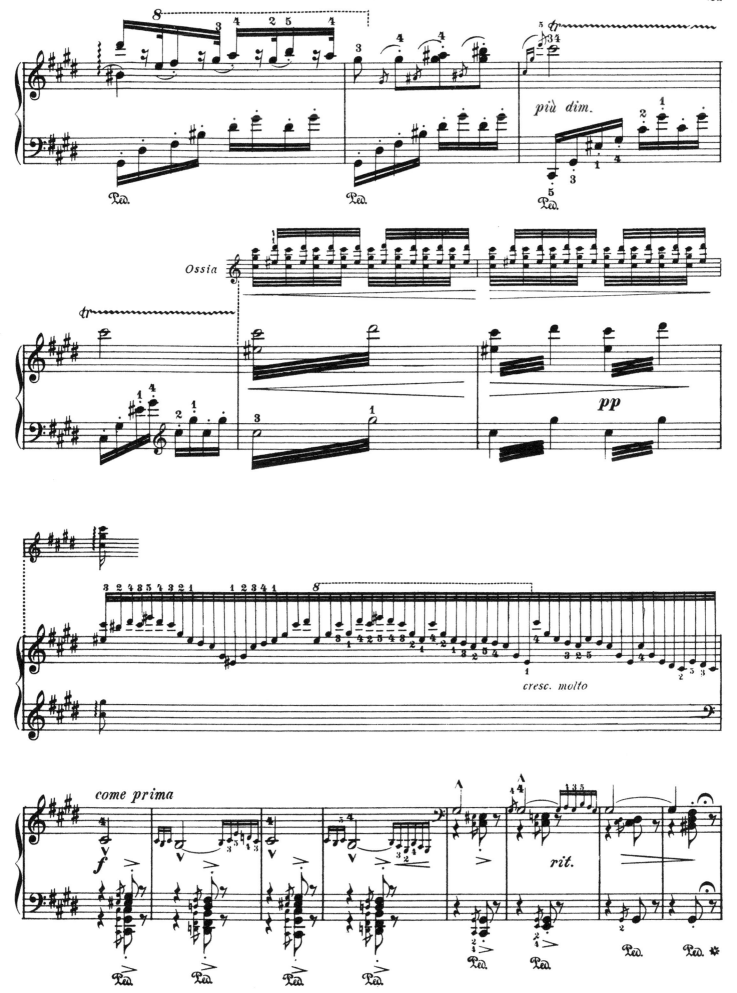

Friska

Prestissimo

Au Comte Leo Festetics

Rhapsodie hongroise № 3

Edited and revised by
Rafael Joseffy

Fr. Liszt

Copyright, 1908, by G. Schirmer, Inc.
Newly-revised Edition
Copyright, 1914, by G. Schirmer, Inc.

Printed in the U. S. A.

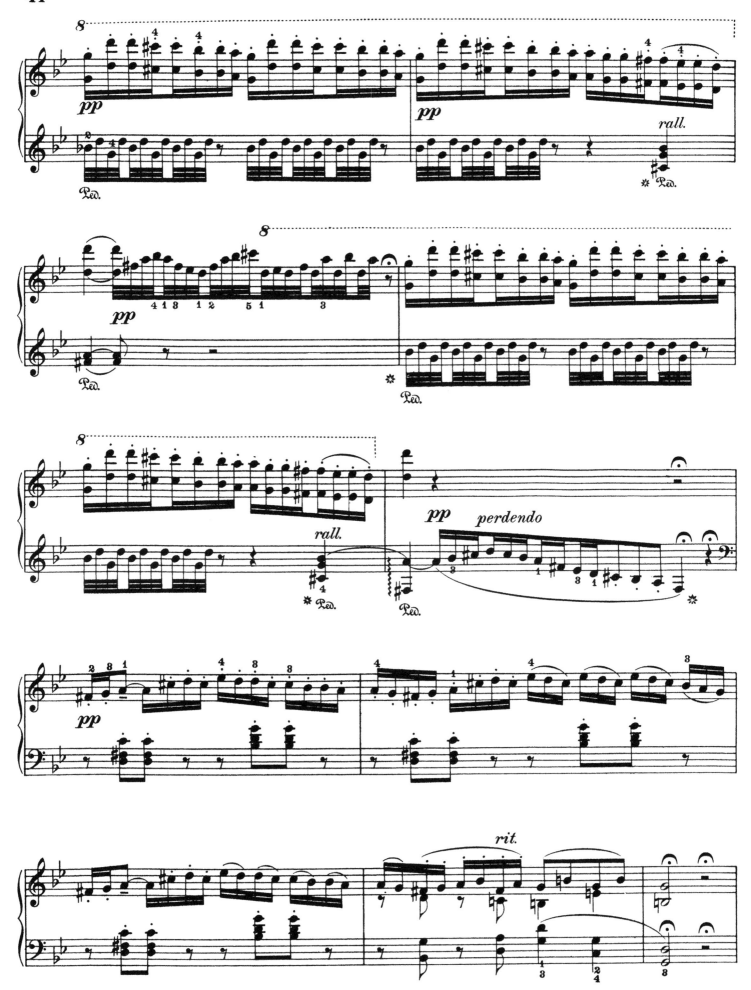

Au Comte Casimir Esterházy

Rhapsodie hongroise N°4

Edited and revised by
Rafuel Joseffy

Fr. Liszt

Quasi adagio, altieramente

Copyright, 1908, by G. Schirmer, Inc. Printed in the U.S.A. Newly-revised Edition
Copyright, 1914, by G. Schirmer, Inc.

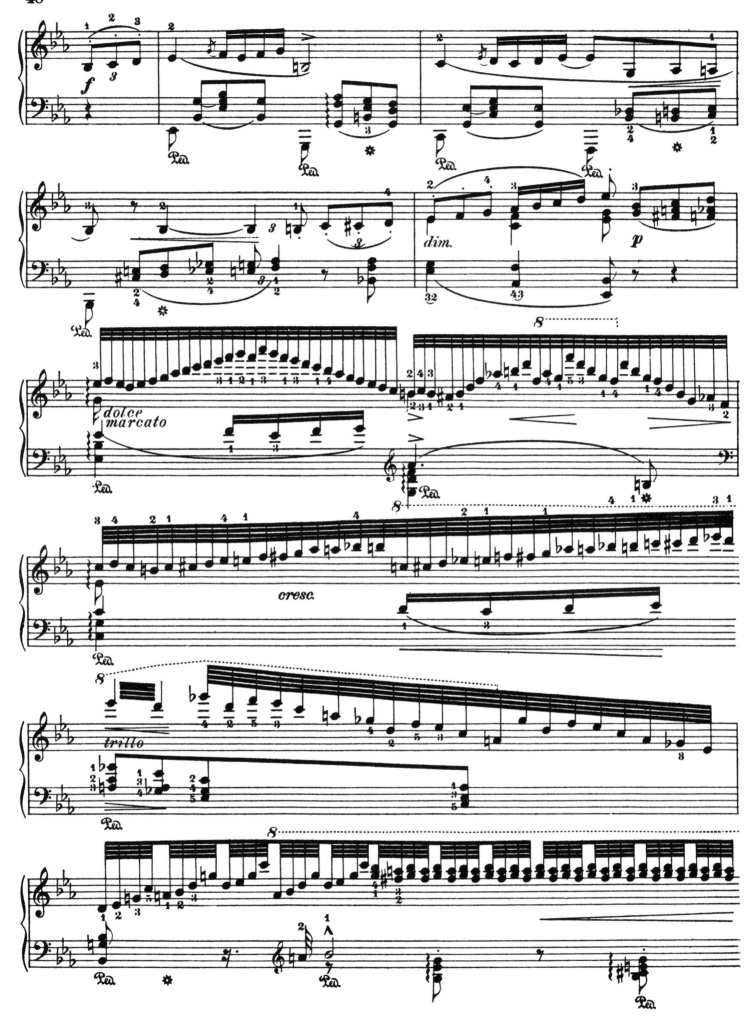

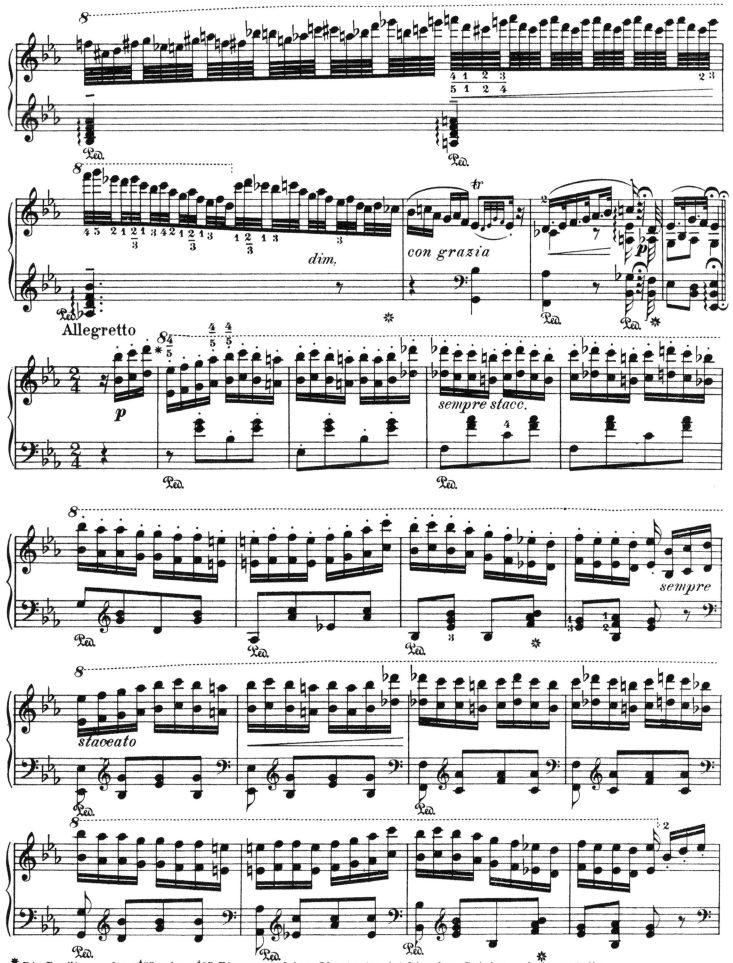

* Die Benützung des 5ten oder 4ten Fingers auf den Obertasten ist hier dem Spieler anheimgestellt.
Here the player may take either the 5th finger or the 4th, as he pleases, on the black keys.

A Madame la Comtesse Sidonie Reviczky

Rhapsodie hongroise № 5
Héroïde élégiaque

Edited and revised by
Rafael Joseffy

Fr. Liszt

Copyright, 1908, by G. Schirmer, Inc. Printed in the U.S.A. Copyright, 1914, by G. Schirmer, Inc.
Newly-revised Edition

dolce con intimo sentimento

Au Comte Antoine d'Appony

Rhapsodie hongroise № 6

Edited and fingered by
Rafael Joseffy

FRANZ LISZT

Copyright renewal assigned, 1930, to G. Schirmer (Inc.)
Copyright, 1902, by G. Schirmer (Inc.)   Printed in the U. S. A.   Newly-revised Edition
Copyright, 1914, by G. Schirmer (Inc.)

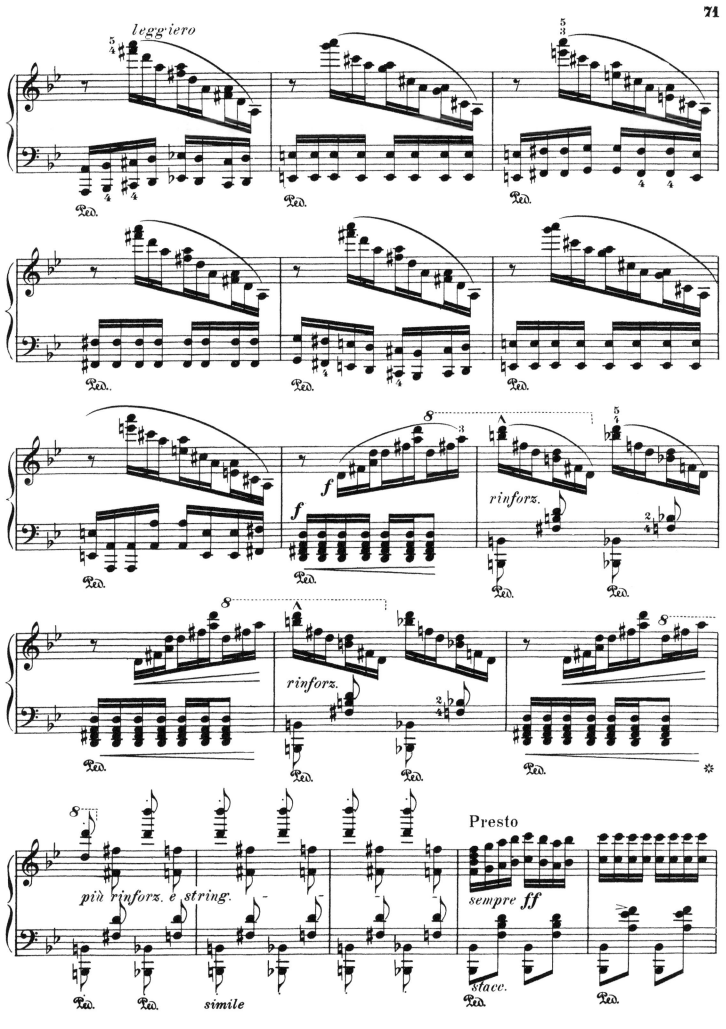

Au Baron Fery Orczy

Rhapsodie hongroise No 7

Edited and revised by
Rafael Joseffy

To be played in the bold, intense Gypsy style

Lento Im trotzigen, tiefsinnigen Zigeuner-Styl vorzutragen

Fr. Liszt

Copyright, 1908, by G. Schirmer, Inc. Printed in the U.S.A. Newly-revised Edition Copyright, 1914, by G. Schirmer, Inc.

A Monsieur A.d'Augusz

Rhapsodie hongroise № 8

Edited and revised by
Rafael Joseffy

Fr. Liszt

Printed in the U. S. A.
Copyright, 1908, by G. Schirmer, Inc.
Newly-revised Edition
Copyright, 1914, by G. Schirmer, Inc.

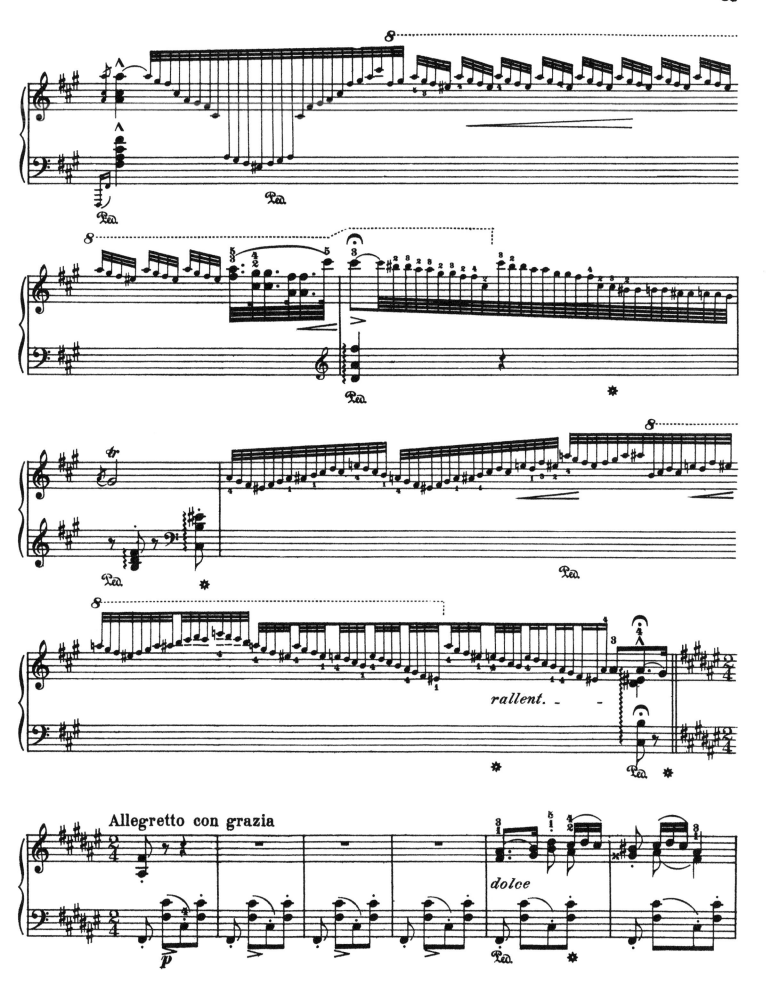

* Der obere, characteristische Fingersatz von Liszt ist schwieriger.

* The characteristic upper fingering, by Liszt, is the more difficult.

poco a poco più animando

cresc.